Zip & Zap Take a Nap

Story by **Christine Ann Gowey**

Illustrated by **Andi Kleinman**

with a Special Message from **Dr. Brandie Gowey, NMD**

Zip & Zap Take a Nap

© 2014 Christine Gowey, Andi Kleinman, Brandie Gowey
All rights reserved. No part of this book may be reproduced or distributed in any form or by any means without the prior written permission of the author.

Published by
DR. DNA Press
Flagstaff, AZ

ISBN: 978-1-947652-10-1

Nation of Publication: United States of America

Proceeds from the sale of this book benefit medical research at DR. DNA Clinic.

Learn more at *goweyresearchgroup.com*.

> The authors of this Work are not dispensing medical or life advice, or prescribing any treatment or technique, for any reason. This Work is merely intended to entertain and inspire thought-provoking discussions of life among adults and children alike. This Work is only intended to provide inspiration and information, and as such, the authors of this Work assume no responsibility for your actions.

Dedication

To my daughter Brandie,
who believed that at age 60,
I could become a published author.
Anything is possible!

Credits

Edited by
Dr. Brandie Gowey, NMD
Linda Todd
Emily Adkins
Phil Brooks
Dianna Hales
Olga Chararrie

Cover & Book Design by
Andi Kleinman

ZIP and ZAP, brothers indeed.
From early on everyone knew they were from the same family.

When the two bees flew together there was no doubt of family *resemblance* with their

steady eyes,

perfect wing span,

and dive.

The love they shared between each other was *unmistakable*.

ZIP woke up with the sunlight each day after a good night's sleep. There were no alarm clocks for him!

He would go out for an early morning *flight* as the sun was warming the earth. *ZIP* was peppy... and the *buzz* was all about him.

ZAP, on the other hand, had an alarm clock that rang and rang. Rolling out of his cubby to start his day was difficult.

He never slept well and was always tired.

After his morning *flight*, ZIP came home for a good breakfast. It was always healthy.

A little yoga and a swim followed before he flew off to work.

Every evening he lifted weights and then had some quiet time.

ZAP never ate breakfast. He didn't have much interest in food.

But he liked to play! In fact, he liked to play too hard and too much! After work every day, he was off to

piano lessons,

soccer,

flight lessons...

... and anything else he could fit in!

ZIP enjoyed each day. He loved the smell of the blossoms on the apple and pear trees. ZIP knew his job would help the trees grow beautiful fruit.

Each day, when he was done, he *hovered* and *admired* his work.
It always made him feel good.

ZAP, however, loved to *buzz* and *twirl* through the air all day long!

But afterward, he felt even more *fatigued*.

Noticing ZAP's busy life, ZIP said, "I'm going to take you to see Dr. B. She's a great doctor and I believe she can help you."

ZAP had no interest in seeing a doctor, but ZIP took him by the hand and off they flew to Dr. B's clinic. He knew it was important to help his brother.

ZIP hovered peacefully as they waited

ZAP continued to fly back and forth, pacing.

"Good morning!" Dr. B greeted the two. "Hmmm," Dr. B continued, "I see from your chart, ZAP, that you're a very busy bee. You'll need to slow down a little."

In a calm, *reassuring* voice Dr. B said, "Perhaps you could start by doing less extra activities, ZAP, and not watch TV or play video games right before bedtime. And turn off loud music when you're trying to go to sleep."

Dr. B went on to explain about how a too-busy life could affect ZAP's *adrenal glands*, body and mood.

The two brothers looked at each other
and knew there would need to be changes.

ZIP was pleased and understood... as did ZAP.

"Thank you, Dr. B! We're going home now," ZIP *buzzed*.
"Okay brother," ZAP *chimed* in.

The two took off into the sky.

When they got back to the *hive*, ZAP looked at ZIP and *suggested*, "Let's play a quiet game of "Sleeping Blossom"… have some honey tea… and then, ZIP, let's take a nap!"

Vocabulary

admired: respected and saw the work well done

adrenal glands: special glands above your kidneys

buzz: 1) fly around quickly making a *buzzing* sound and 2) excited talk

chimed: spoke at the same time or added to the conversation

fatigued: weak and too tired to function normally

flight: flying through the air using wings

hive: a home for bees

hormones: chemicals your body makes that affect how your body works

hovered: flew and floated about in the air

immune system: how your body protects you from diseases

nutrients: the good stuff in food that your body uses to keep you healthy

reassuring: being made to feel everything will be all right

resemblance: look alike or similar to

suggested: hinted

twirl: to swing, fly and roll in a circle

unmistakable: very obvious

A Special Message from Dr. B

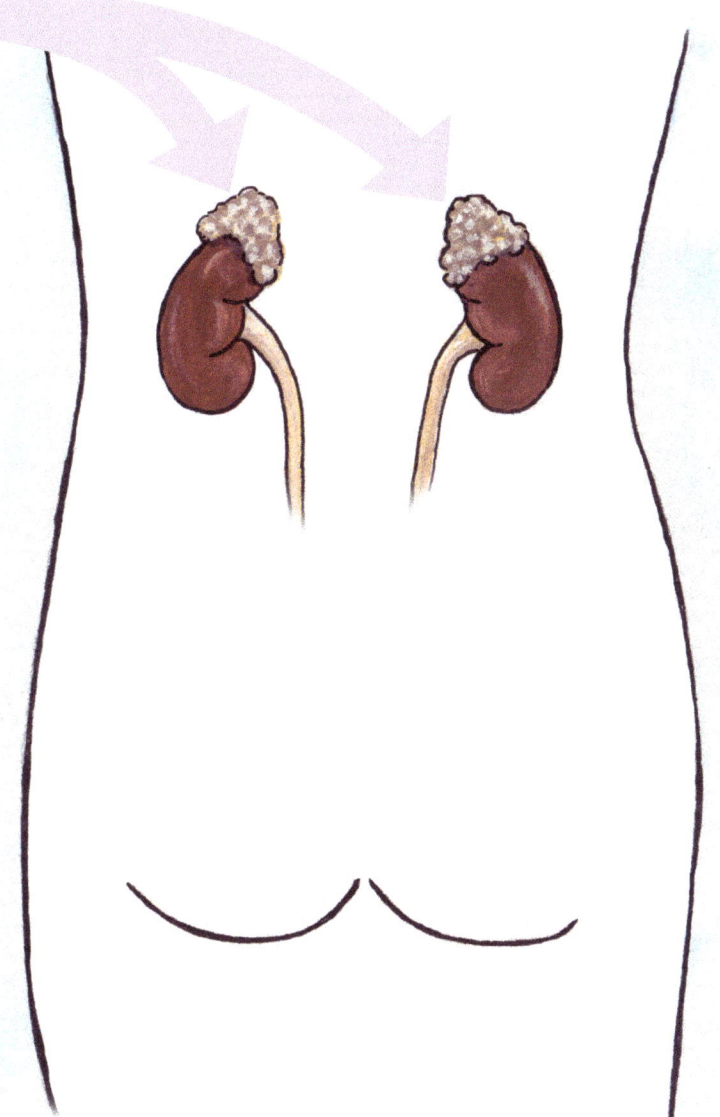

Adrenal glands are a very important part of your body. You have two of them. They sit above your kidneys near the middle part of your back.

Adrenal glands produce *hormones*. These *hormones* help your body with many things. They give you energy, stimulate your appetite and make you feel sleepy at bedtime. They also help your body get *nutrients* from the food you eat and they regulate your *immune system*, which helps your body fight off sickness—like a cold or the flu.

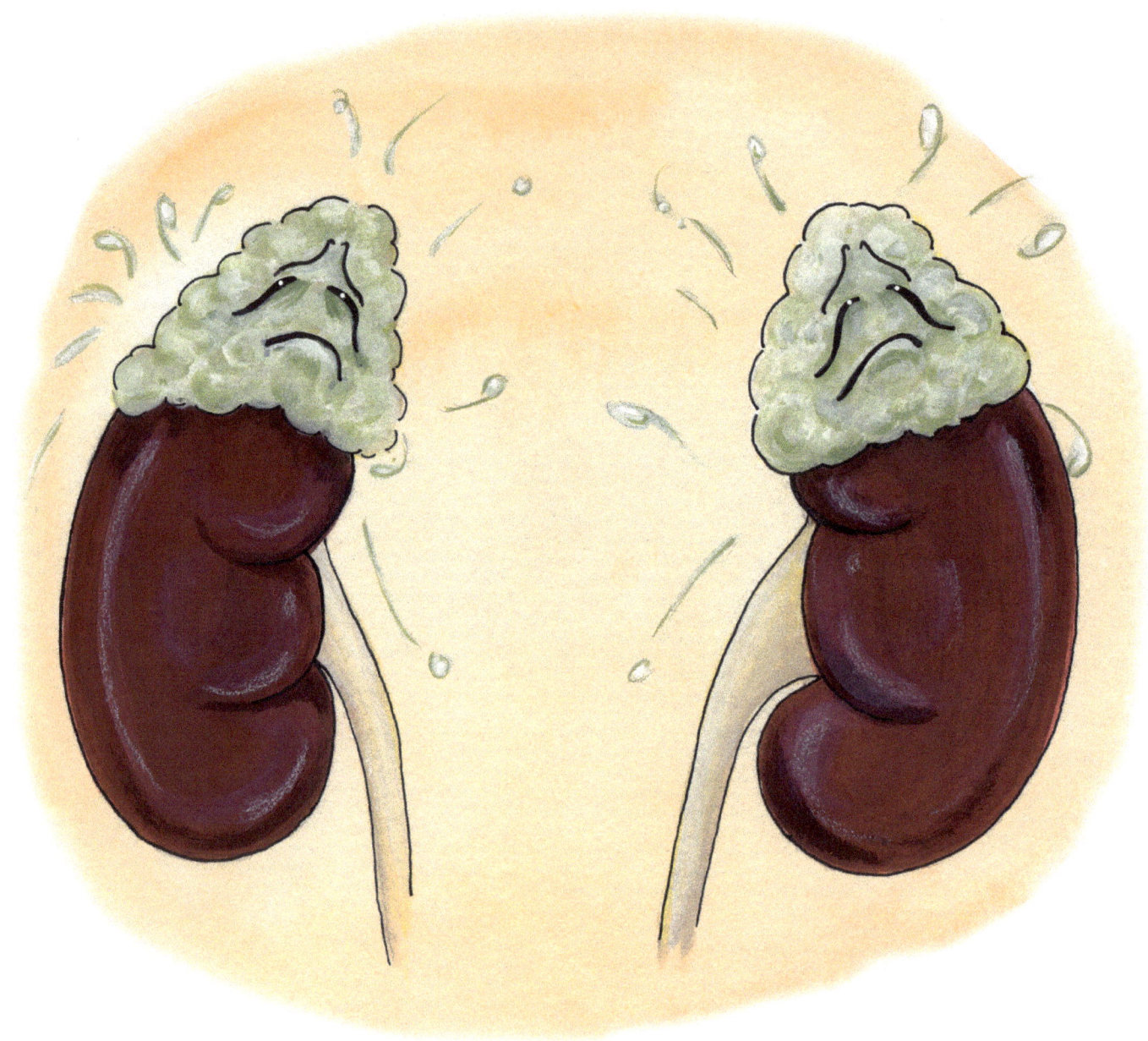

Sometimes, when you become too busy… or don't eat well… or don't rest enough… these glands become very tired and their ability to make *hormones* changes.

You may start to feel bad (not like your normal self) and, like ZAP in the story,

you may have a hard time getting out of bed in the morning...

... or you may get sick a lot...

... or have a short temper.

Follow ZIP's example to keep your adrenal glands healthy—

Rest.

Enjoy your life
one moment at a time.

Take time for quiet.

Eat well—
lots of veggies, good protein and some fruit.

Get a good night's sleep.

If you do these things you will feel much better!

Read this book with your parents and work together to take better care of your *adrenal glands*. If you follow Dr. B's *suggestions* and still do not feel well, you know what to do…

"Call Dr. B!"

To find a Naturopathic doctor near you, go to **naturopathic.org**.